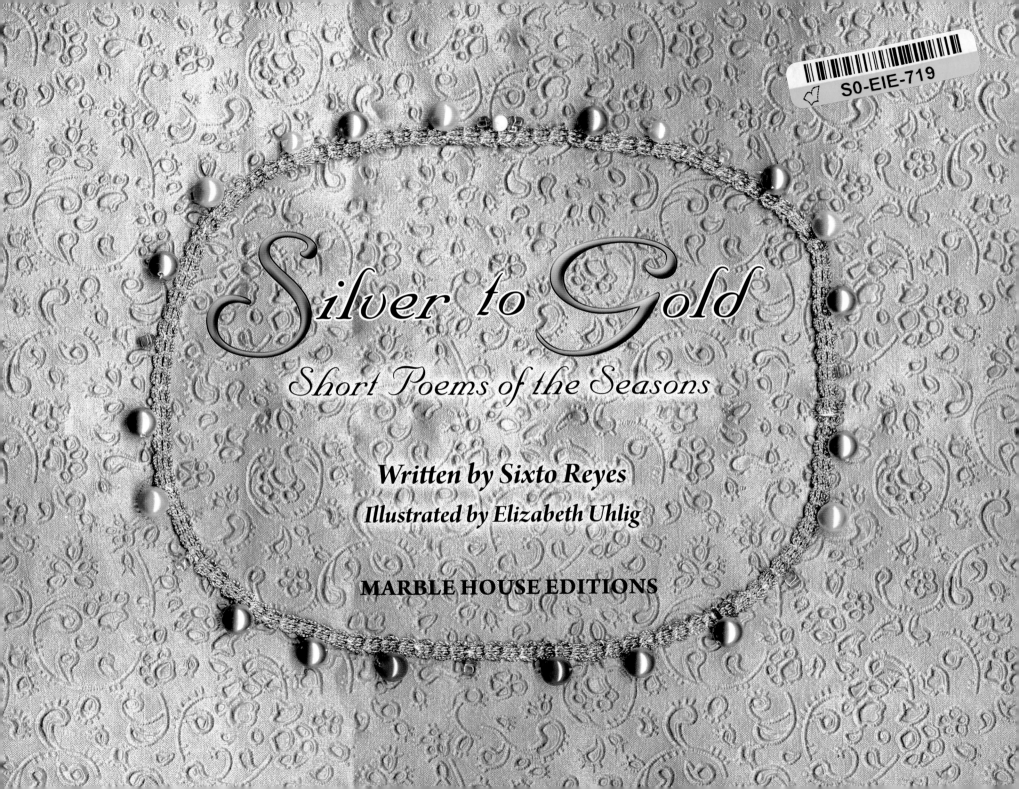

Silver to Gold

Short Poems of the Seasons

Written by Sixto Reyes

Illustrated by Elizabeth Uhlig

MARBLE HOUSE EDITIONS

Published by Marble House Editions
96-09 66th Avenue (Suite 1D)
Rego Park, NY 11374
elizabeth.uhlig@yahoo.com
www.marble-house-editions.com

Library of Congress Cataloguing-in-Publication Data
Reyes, Sixto
Silver to Gold/ by Sixto Reyes

Summary: Four illustrated sets of short poems reflecting the four seasons.

Production Date   October 2011
Plant & Location   Printed by Everbest Printing Co. Ltd., Nansha, China
Job & Batch #   102427

ISBN 978-0-9834030-1-2
Library of Congress Catalog Card Number 2001012345

To my favorite teacher, my wife Eileen,
who enlightens me daily with her wisdom.

Winter

Slender shards of light
Spill over the horizon.
A new day . . .

Cold and hard
Driven by the northeast winds
Sleet like razors fell.

Suspended
Against the slate grey sky
Origami gulls.

Winter's hasty thaw
Impromptu streams converge
Along the stone walk.

Spring

Eager crocus . . .
Like baby fingers, pokes
Through Earth's moist cake.

Minnows congregate
In great numbers
Along the water's edge.

Through pavement's fissure

Slender tendrils grow

Wild summer blossoms.

Long swaying rows
Of cherry and dogwood
A pink and white parade.

Summer

Swift flowing stream
Creates wistful melodies
Over smooth green stones.

High June sun
Brisk noon breeze
Tree shadows dance.

Hovering lightly
Above pale yellow pistils
Rapid wings delight.

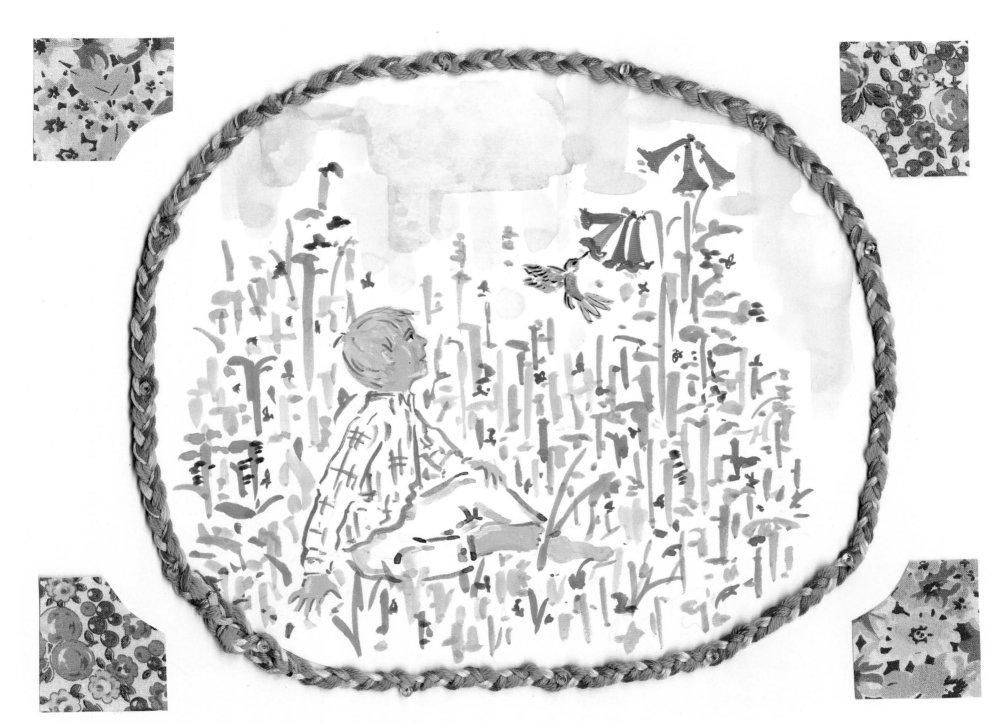

The morning shower
Leaves a full summer bouquet
Scents of red and blue.

Fall

A seed on the wind

carries possibilities

of diverse landscapes.

Crisp autumn orchard
In full September splendor
Yields her new bounty.

November leaves dance
Pirouetting on the ground
Amidst wind and rain.

Wind prods drying leaves
Cacophony of crickets
The last acorn drops.

THE END